Living with Nature

About Wise & Wide

- A systematic 6-level English reading program based on Lexile® measures
- Diverse and interesting topics chosen from the elementary curriculums of Korea and English speaking western countries
- Well-written books in various forms including fiction stories, descriptive texts, and classics retold
- The informative but original fiction stories grab your interest, leading to the easy and clear understanding of the educational content.
- Improve thinking skills with solid after-reading activities at all levels of the series.

Wise & Wide is a 6-level English reading program that consists of 60 books and each level is systematically divided by Lexile® measures. The Lexile® Framework for Reading is the most popular reading measuring system in American formal education curriculums and many English programs. Over 20 out of 50 states in the U.S. mark Lexile® measures directly on students' final report cards and over 300 well-known publishers adopt and use Lexile® measures.

Experience many kinds of readings written by professional writers from the U.S. and England. They used interesting topics that were carefully chosen after analyzing elementary curriculums from around the world including Korea, the U.S., England, and Australia among many others. Comprehensive after-reading activities including graphic organizers, speaking tasks, and After-reading Tests are ready for you.

Levels in the series and their corresponding Lexile® measures

Level	Lexile® measures	U.S. Grade
Level 1	Below 200L	Pre K - K
Level 2	190L - 400L	Lower Grade 1
Level 3	350L - 530L	Upper Grade 1
Level 4	420L - 650L	Grade 2
Level 5	520L - 940L	Grade 3 - 4
Level 6	830L - 1070L	Grade 5 - 6

* Smart Readers: Wise & Wide level 1 is applicable to the preschool level in the U.S.
* The source of the relationship between Lexile® measures and U.S. school grades: CCSS(Common Core State Standards) FOR ENGLISH LANGUAGE ARTS, APPENDIX A (2012, which is used by 45 states in the U.S.)

Topic List

	Level 1	Level 2	Level 3	Level 4	Level 5	Level 6
Book 1	Science>Biology: The hibernation of animals Story	Science>Biology: Living and nonliving things Story	Science>Biology> Animals & the Environment: Sea otters Story	Environment> Living with nature: The diver & the persimmon tree Story	Science>Biology> Animal: Amazing animals of the Amazon Story	Science>Biology: Germs, transmitted diseases Story
Book 2	Literature> World classics: Aesop's fables Story	Literature> Traditional fairy tale: Old tales about stones Story	Social Studies> Economy: To run a business to make and save money Story	Science>Biology> Plants: Photosynthesis Story	Science>Earth science: Earth's layers, earthquakes, volcanoes, and earth's atmosphere Report	Mathematics> Sequence: The golden ratio & the Fibonacci sequence Story
Book 3	Science>Physics: How shadows are formed Story	Literature> World classics: Peter Pan Story	Science>Scientific technology: Nanobots Story	Literature>Myths: World's creation stories Story	Literature> Legend: The story of King Arthur Story	
Book 4	Literature> Traditional literature: The Talmud Story	Science>Biology> Animal: Polar bears Story	Science>Biology> Animal: Mountain gorillas Story	Social Studies> Cultural anthropology: Amazing ancient cultures of the world Story	Science> Earth science: Clouds and weather Story	
Book 5			Social Studies> Cultural anthropology: Astonishing festivals Report	Art>Music: Stories from two operas Story		
Book 6				Social Studies> People: Three great people who overcame hardships Story		
Book 7						
Book 8						
Book 9						
Book 10						

* 10 books in each level will be published.

How to Use This Book

• Before Reading

You can easily find the topic and what kind of story you are about to read.

• The text

All the stories were written by professional writers from the U.S. and England, so you will read authentic and appropriate English sentences and expressions in every book in the series.

• Pop Quiz

Check out right away if you understand what you have just read by solving a pop quiz that checks your comprehension.

• Key Words

The key words and expressions on each page are listed for you to easily study them.

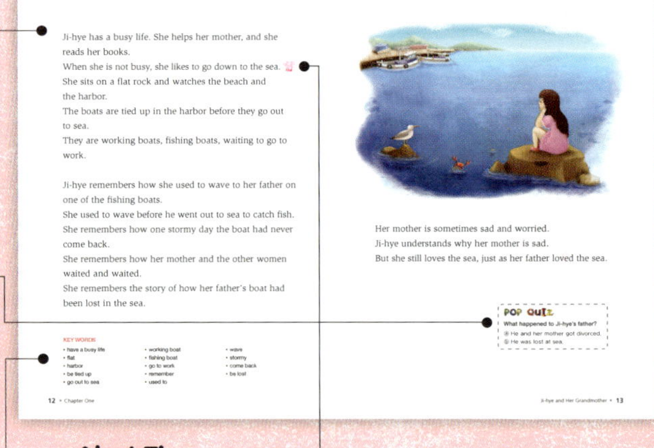

• Aha! Tips

Download free Korean explanations at *www.ihappyhouse.co.kr* for all of the sentences marked with "Aha!". These explain cultural, scientific, and economic knowledge or they deal with aspects of English such as grammatical structures or idiomatic expressions. There are lots of "Aha! Tips" to help you understand the text.

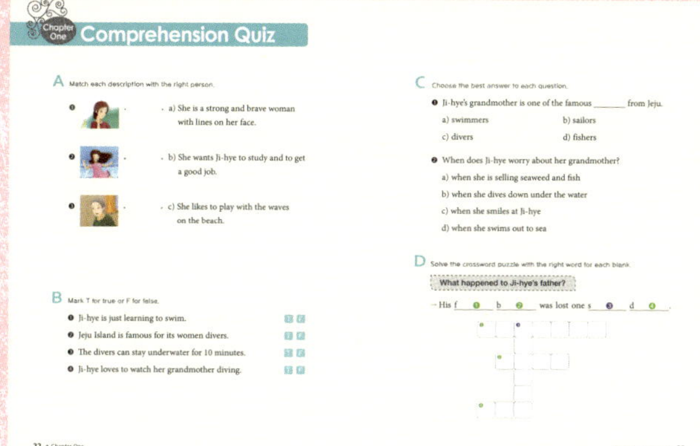

•Comprehension Quiz

After reading one chapter, solve various questions to find out if you fully understand the content.

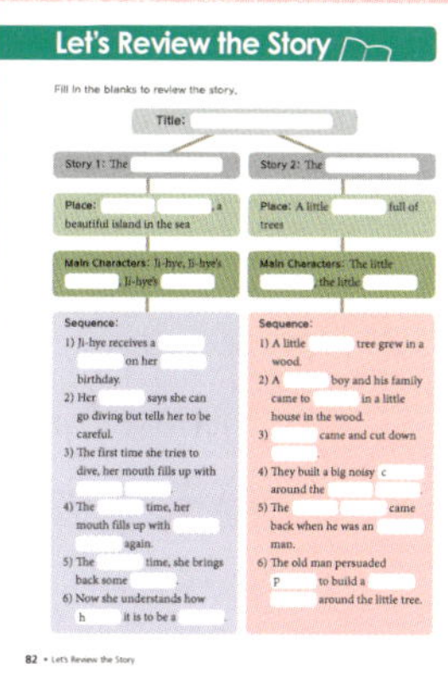 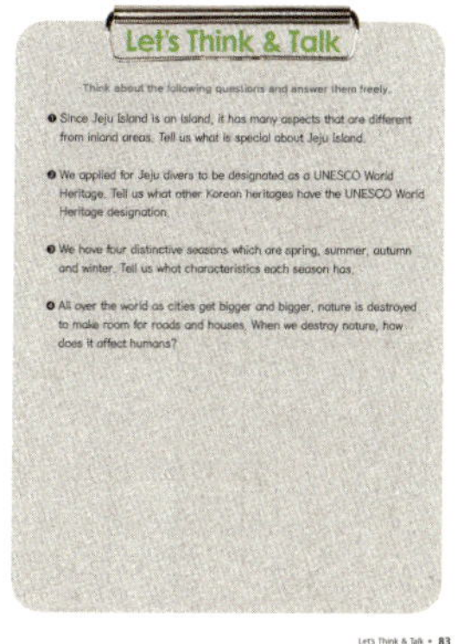

•Let's Review the Story /
•Let's Think & Talk

Fill in the blanks in the organizer to summarize the whole story. Express your own thinking and feelings about the story by answering the questions. You can build up logic and reasoning skills for your essay examinations in the future.

Appendix 

Audio CD

In the CD audio book form, the texts are read vividly by American professional voice actors.

After-reading Test

Solve an additionally provided After-reading Test for each book.

The Korean translation, Answer Keys, a Word Quiz, a Word List, and Aha! Tips for each book

You can download them for free at *www.ihappyhouse.co.kr*

Before Reading

Living with Nature

Level 4-1, Lexile® 570L

•Environment > Living with nature
•Story

Living with nature

The earth, sea, and sky are part of nature as are plants, trees, and flowers. All of those are part of nature and humans and animals also belong to nature. In other words, we are always with nature.

Without nature, we humans couldn't exist. However, many people who live in cities often forget the existence of nature. Let's explore nature itself and our relationship with nature through The Persimmon Tree and The Grandmother Diver. Let's check out how a pretty persimmon tree is in harmony with its surroundings and how it goes through the four seasons and what the life of a Jeju diver is like.

The Grandmother Diver

Ji-hye is a girl who lives on Jeju Island. She loves the sea and her dream is to become a diver. Therefore, she always watches carefully her grandmother and her grandmother's friends who are divers. Meanwhile, Ji-hye's mother who lost her husband in the sea is very worried that Ji-hye may become a diver. On her eighth birthday, Ji-hye gets a diving suit for her birthday present. Can she dive well?

The Persimmon Tree

In a pretty forest where many trees and animals live, a persimmon seed falls to the ground. The persimmon seed sprouts and grows into a beautiful persimmon tree. Every autumn, it is laden with shiny and delicious persimmons. One day,

some people come to the forest and cut down trees and built a house. Then, one family moves into the house. The persimmon tree becomes a friend to a kid from the family and has a happy life. But this time, a big city is built around the persimmon tree. What will happen to the persimmon tree?

Contents

Living with Nature

The Grandmother Diver

Ji-hye and Her Grandmother

Ji-hye lives on an island in the sea. It is a beautiful island called Jeju Island.

The sun shines every day. The sky is always blue.

Many people visit the island for their holidays.

When a man and a woman get married, they go on a holiday.

This holiday is called a honeymoon.

Many men and women go to Jeju Island for their honeymoon.

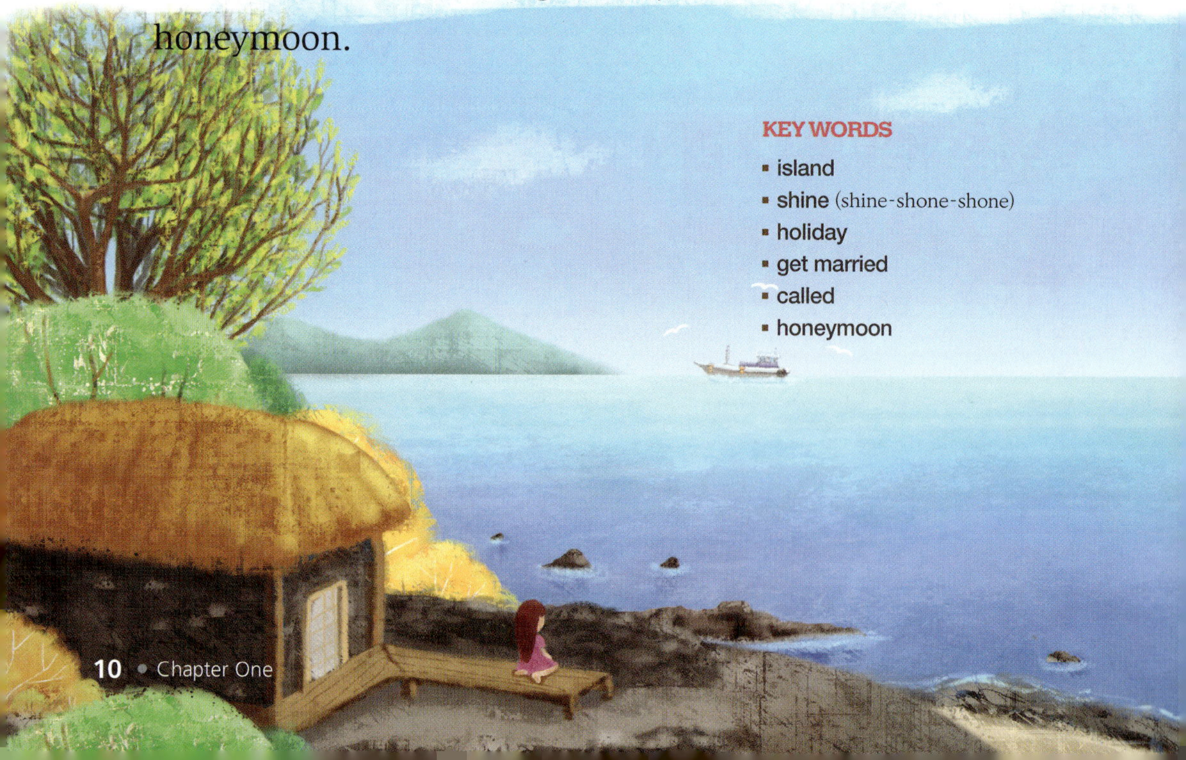

KEY WORDS

- island
- shine (shine-shone-shone)
- holiday
- get married
- called
- honeymoon

But Ji-hye lives on Jeju Island all of the time, not just
during holidays.

Ji-hye is seven years old. She lives with her mother and
grandmother. They live in a small house close to the sea.
When Ji-hye looks out from her house, she can see
the sea.

She loves to sit outside her house, and watch the sea.
She watches the birds. The birds fly over the shore and
dive into the water.

She watches the boats. The boats sail out to sea and
look for fish.

Sometimes she just watches the waves of the sea coming
in and going out.

KEY WORDS

- close to
- shore
- dive into
- sail
- look for
- wave

Ji-hye has a busy life. She helps her mother, and she reads her books.

When she is not busy, she likes to go down to the sea.

She sits on a flat rock and watches the beach and the harbor.

The boats are tied up in the harbor before they go out to sea.

They are working boats, fishing boats, waiting to go to work.

Ji-hye remembers how she used to wave to her father on one of the fishing boats.

She used to wave before he went out to sea to catch fish.

She remembers how one stormy day the boat had never come back.

She remembers how her mother and the other women waited and waited.

She remembers the story of how her father's boat had been lost in the sea.

KEY WORDS

- have a busy life
- flat
- harbor
- be tied up
- go out to sea
- working boat
- fishing boat
- go to work
- remember
- used to
- wave
- stormy
- come back
- be lost

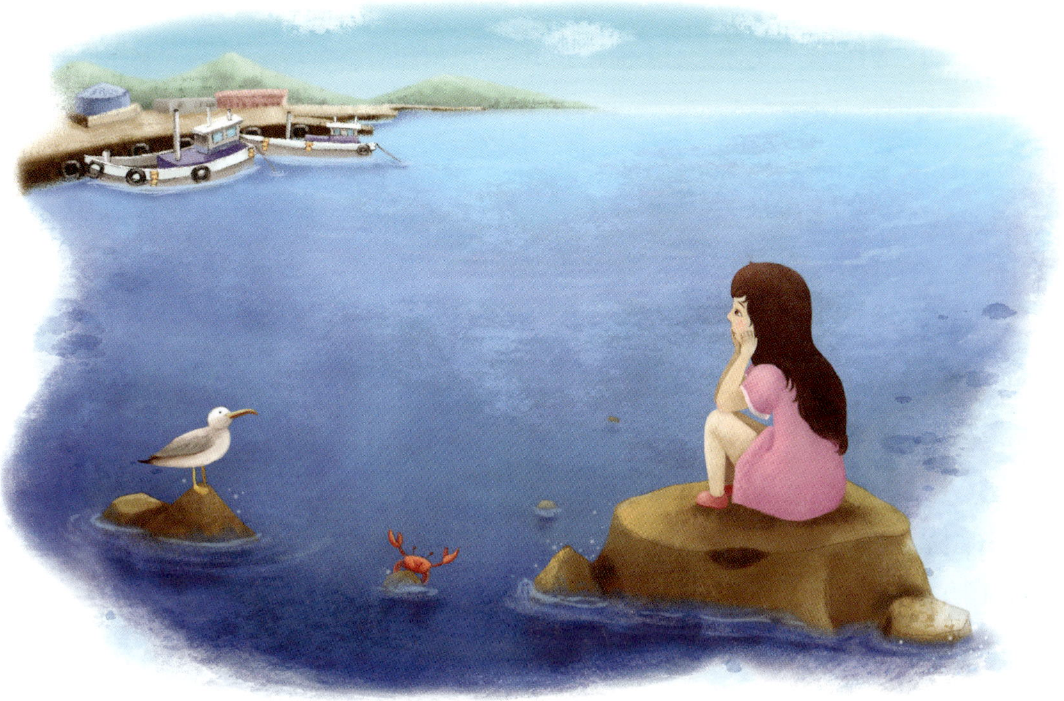

Her mother is sometimes sad and worried.
Ji-hye understands why her mother is sad.
But she still loves the sea, just as her father loved the sea.

POP QUIZ

What happened to Ji-hye's father?

ⓐ He and her mother got divorced.
ⓑ He was lost at sea.

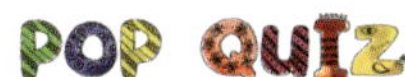

Later, when the boats are full of fish, they come back
to the harbor.
Ji-hye watches the sailors.
They pour the wriggling silver fish into big wooden boxes.
Ji-hye loves the sea.
She likes to play with the waves where they come onto
the beach.

KEY WORDS

- be full of
- sailor
- pour
- wriggle
- come onto the beach
- go into
- faster
- learn
- call A B
- quickly
- through
- diver

She goes into the water and waits for a big wave.
Then, she runs onto the beach and tries to run faster
than the wave.
She learned to swim when she was very young.
Her friends call her "Ji-hye the Fish."
She swims quickly through the water with her arms and
legs wriggling.

Ji-hye's favorite time is when she is watching her
grandmother and all of her grandmother's friends.
Ji-hye's grandmother is a diver. The women divers of
Jeju Island are famous.

POP QUIZ

Find three verbs describing what Ji-hye does.

ⓐ She r ___________ faster than the waves.
ⓑ She s ___________ like a fish.
ⓒ She w ___________ her arms and legs.

The divers swim out from the beach.

They dive under the water to find seaweed and fish.

They can dive for two minutes before they come up for air.

They are strong and brave women with lines on their faces.

Everyone knows about the divers. They are famous all around the world.

It is only on Jeju Island that there are women like Ji-hye's grandmother.

There have been women divers there for hundreds of years.

They dive to get seaweed and fish.

When they come back, they sit by the sea and sell what they have caught.

Ji-hye's mother helps them to sell, too. But she never goes into the sea.

Ji-hye watches them most days. She knows all of the divers, and they know her.

KEY WORDS

- **find** (find-found-found)
- **seaweed**
- **come up for air**
- **brave**

- **line**
- **all around the world**
- **hundreds of**
- **like**

- **sell**
- **catch** (catch-caught-caught)
- **most days**
- **dangerous**

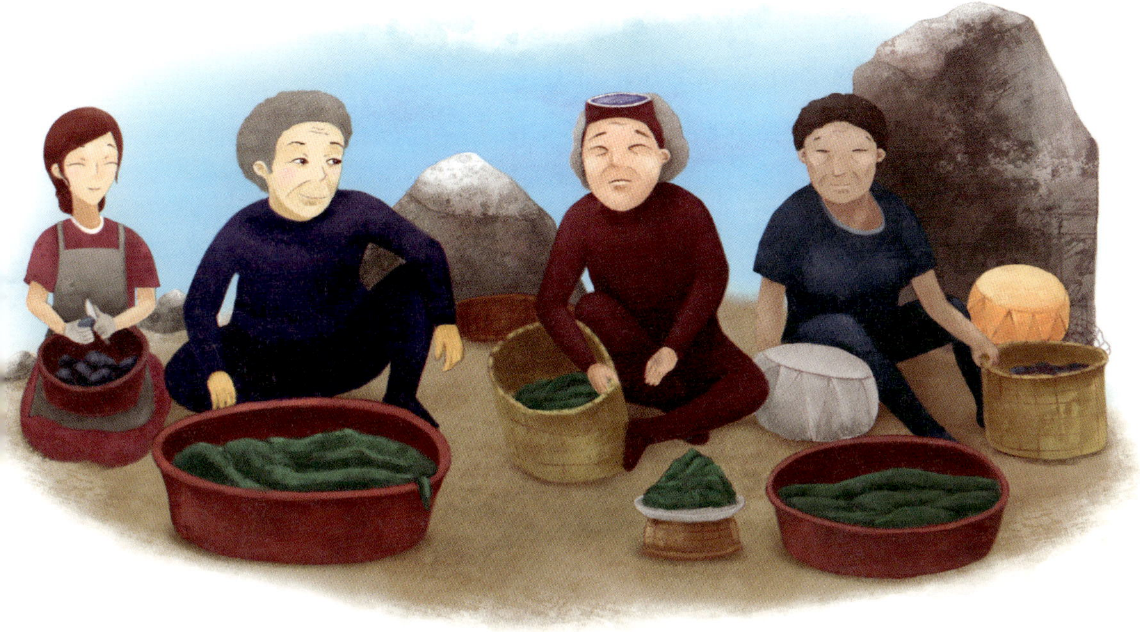

The divers do not smile very often. Their work is hard and dangerous.

But they always smile when they see Ji-hye.

POP QUIZ

What does Ji-hye's mother do?

ⓐ She goes fishing on a boat.

ⓑ She sells seaweed and fish.

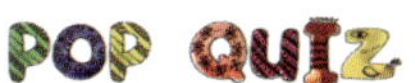

Ji-hye watches her grandmother going into the water.

She wears a black rubber suit.

She has goggles over her eyes to keep out the water.

She has big fins on her feet to help her swim fast.

She has a belt with heavy weights on it.

The belt helps her to get down to the bottom of the sea.

She carries a big float with a net that she can put things in.

Ji-hye watches her grandmother swim far out to sea.
She goes out when the moon says that the tide is right. 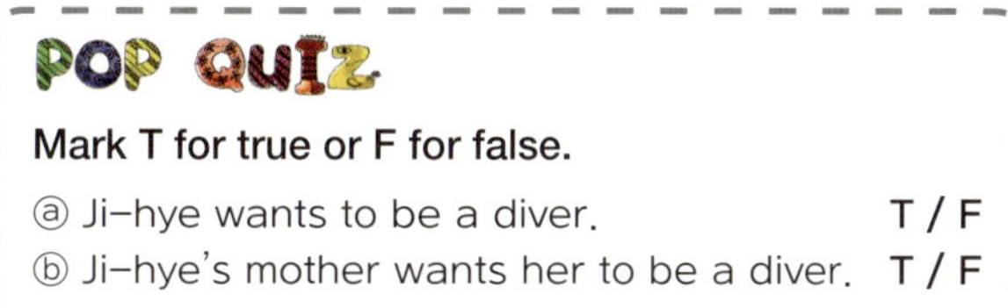
She swims far out to sea. There is more seaweed, and
there are more fish far out at sea.
Ji-hye can see her grandmother's head going up and
down in the water as she swims.
When she gets to the right place, she ties her float. She
dives down into the water.

POP QUIZ

Mark T for true or F for false.
ⓐ Ji-hye wants to be a diver.   T / F
ⓑ Ji-hye's mother wants her to be a diver.   T / F

▲ a big float with a net

KEY WORDS

- rubber suit
- goggles
- keep out (keep-kept-kept)
- fin

- weight
- get down to
- bottom
- float with a net

- tide
- up and down
- get to (get-got-gotten)
- tie

Ji-hye cannot see her grandmother while she is under the water.

Every time this happens, Ji-hye worries a little.

But when her grandmother comes back up, she can see her again.

Ji-hye waves, but no one ever waves back.

The divers are too busy and too far away.

Ji-hye dreams that one day she will be a diver like
her grandmother.

But her mother always says that being a diver is too hard.

She wants Ji-hye to study so that she can have a better

job.

She says that her grandmother has worked hard so that
Ji-hye will not have to work so hard.

A Match each description with the right person.

❶  •

❷  •

❸  •

a) She is a strong and brave woman with lines on her face.

b) She wants Ji-hye to study and to get a good job.

c) She likes to play with the waves on the beach.

B Mark T for true or F for false.

❶ Ji-hye is just learning to swim. T F

❷ Jeju Island is famous for its women divers. T F

❸ The divers can stay underwater for 10 minutes. T F

❹ Ji-hye loves to watch her grandmother diving. T F

Choose the best answer to each question.

❶ Ji-hye's grandmother is one of the famous _________ from Jeju.

a) swimmers

b) sailors

c) divers

d) fishers

❷ When does Ji-hye worry about her grandmother?

a) when she is selling seaweed and fish

b) when she dives down under the water

c) when she smiles at Ji-hye

d) when she swims out to sea

D Solve the crossword puzzle with the right word for each blank.

> **What happened to Ji-hye's father?**

→ His f __❶__ b __❷__ was lost one s __❸__ d __❹__ .

Ji-hye's Birthday

One day, Ji-hye wakes up very early. She is excited.

It is her birthday. She is eight years old. Her mother has promised her a special day.

After Ji-hye's mother and grandmother wake up, they eat rice and seaweed soup.

Ji-hye's mother brings her a present. It is a big book of maps.

There are maps of every country in the world.

But there is another present too.

This present is too big to be another book.

Ji-hye takes the paper off the present. She looks to see what is inside.

KEY WORDS

- **wake up** (wake-woke-woken)
- **excited**
- **promise**
- **too ~ to…**
- **take off** (take-took-taken)
- **inside**
- **underneath**
- **a pair of**
- **rush**
- **put on** (put-put-put)
- **swimsuit**
- **hug**

It is a black rubber suit. It is just like her grandmother's suit.

Underneath the suit there are goggles and a pair of fins.

Ji-hye rushes to take off her clothes. She puts on her swimsuit.

Then, she puts on the rubber suit, the goggles, and the fins.

"Look at me," says Ji-hye. "I am a diver, just like Grandmother."

Ji-hye loves her suit, and she hugs her mother and her grandmother.

"Now you have your own suit and goggles. You look just like me," says Ji-hye's grandmother. "Would you like to go diving with me too?"

Ji-hye looks at her mother.
"Can I go with her?" she asks. "Please."
Ji-hye's mother is worried. She has the sad face that Ji-hye knows. Ji-hye knows that she is thinking about her father.

She worries that something bad will happen.
But she can see how much Ji-hye wants to go with her grandmother.

"You can go with her," says Ji-hye's mother. "Perhaps that way you will see just how dangerous the sea can be. But be careful. Do whatever your grandmother tells you to do."

Ji-hye waits while her grandmother changes into
her rubber suit.
She collects her goggles, fins, and float. She has another
float for Ji-hye.
She holds Ji-hye's hand, and they walk down to
the beach.
Ji-hye's mother stays in front of the house and watches
them go.
They get to the beach. Ji-hye's grandmother helps her to
put on her fins.
Then, she puts on her goggles. They walk out into
the sea, carrying their floats.

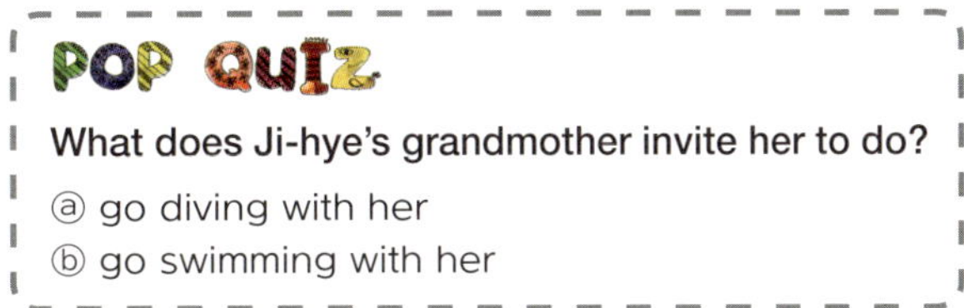

KEY WORDS

- whatever
- change into
- collect

- **hold** (hold-held-held)
- in front of

As they walk into the sea, the water gets deeper and
deeper.

They have to swim. "Ji-hye the Fish" is a good swimmer.

When they are a little way out, her grandmother stops
swimming. She nods her head.

"Here," she says. "Watch me, Ji-hye."

Ji-hye watches her grandmother put her goggles on. She
dives down under the water.

Ji-hye puts her goggles on. She dips her head under
the water.

She can see clearly under the water through her goggles.

She can see seaweed growing at the bottom of the sea.

The seaweed waves as the water moves.

She can see little fish, a crab, and a bright starfish.

She can see her grandmother diving down to the bottom.

She cuts some of the seaweed.

KEY WORDS

- deeper and deeper
- stop + *Verb*-ing
- a little way
- nod
- dive down

- dip
- clearly
- at the bottom of
- crab
- starfish

Her grandmother comes back up into the air.

She puts the seaweed in her net.

Now, it is Ji-hye's chance to dive. Her grandmother holds her hand and pulls her down.

Ji-hye dips down in the water a little way. She pulls at some seaweed.

It does not come free. Ji-hye pulls again, but it is too strong.

She cannot breathe any longer.

She squeezes her grandmother's hand hard.

Ji-hye comes up from under the water.

Her grandmother makes her hold on to the big float.

Her mouth is full of sea water.

Her goggles have filled with water, too.

She spits out the salty water and tries to breathe again.

Her throat is hurting from coughing up the water.

Her eyes are burning too.

KEY WORDS

- chance
- pull down
- pull
- free
- breathe

- squeeze
- not ~ any longer
- hold on to
- fill with
- spit out

- hurt (hurt-hurt-hurt)
- cough up
- burn

For a moment, she is frightened that she will sink under the water.

Her grandmother pats her on the back, so that she can get all of the water out of her body.

"I can't do it, Grandmother. It is too hard," she says sadly.

"Yes, it is hard, but I am sure you will be able to get some seaweed.

You need to keep trying," says her grandmother.

Ji-hye tries again, and again she cannot get any seaweed. Again her mouth fills with water, and she coughs and spits.

Again she is frightened. But she does not want to give up.

For a third time, Ji-hye dives down under the water. This time, a little piece of seaweed comes off in her hand.

She comes back up to the surface. She holds the seaweed up in the air.

Ji-hye calls out to her grandmother. "Look, look, seaweed! I dived for it, and I got it!"

KEY WORDS

- frightened
- **sink** (sink-sank-sunk)
- **pat**
- **get A out of**

- keep + *Verb*-ing
- **cough**
- **give up** (give-gave-given)
- **third**

- come off
- surface
- hold up
- call out

She is so excited. She has done it.

This is her first ever dive to get something from the sea.

She is a diver, just like she has always dreamed.

By the time Ji-hye gets back home with her grandmother, she is tired.

It is much harder than she thought to be a diver.

And this time she did not even swim out very far or dive very deep.

Now she sees just how hard it is. She sees how dangerous swimming and diving in the sea can be.

Her grandmother smiles at her.

"Your mother is right," she says. "The sea can be
a dangerous place. Now you understand that, Ji-hye.
Now you can see just how hard it is to be a diver."
Ji-hye smiles too. "Yes, Grandmother," she says.
Perhaps her mother is right.
Perhaps she will study hard and get a job which is
safer. Aha!
Perhaps she will just watch her grandmother and her
friends diving.

POP QUIZ
Find and write two adjectives to describe diving in the sea.
→ h_______________ , d_______________

KEY WORDS

- by the time
- get back home
- tired
- much harder
- perhaps
- right
- get a job
- safer

Her mother will be happy if that happens.

But for now, Ji-hye will secretly keep her dream alive.

Ji-hye does not have a heavy belt to get down deep in the sea.

She is too young. But in her secret dream, she has a belt.

When she is older, she will get a belt of her own.

Then, she will swim far out to the deeper water or go in a boat.

She will do it when the moon says that the tide is right.

Even if it is only once — to show that she can — she will go to sea like her father did.

She will be a diver like her grandmother. But for now she is happy to dream.

She is happy to collect seaweed with her grandmother in the shallow water near the shore.

KEY WORDS

- for now
- secretly
- alive
- heavy
- of one's own
- once
- shallow
- near

A Write the name of each present Ji–hye received.

❶

❸

❷

B Choose the right word that describes how Ji–hye feels in each case.

happy	tired	excited	frightened

❶ when she wakes up on her birthday → __________________

❷ when she gets her diving suit → __________________

❸ when her mouth fills with sea water → __________________

❹ when she gets back home → __________________

C Choose the best answer to each question.

❶ When is the best time to swim out to the deep water?

    a) in the early morning

    b) at midnight when it is dark

    c) when the moon says the tide is right

    d) at midday when the sun is highest

❷ Why doesn't Ji-hye's mother want her to go diving?

    a) She wants Ji-hye to help cook dinner.

    b) She thinks it is too dangerous.

    c) She thinks her mother is too old to look after her.

    d) She wants to take Ji-hye to buy her a present.

D Put the sentences in order.

❶ Ji-hye's mother let her go.

❷ Ji-hye learned that diving was harder than she had thought.

❸ Ji-hye got a diving suit for her birthday.

❹ Ji-hye's grandmother said she could go diving with her.

________ → ________ → ________ → ________

The Persimmon Tree

The Little Tree

A persimmon is a shiny orange fruit which grows on
a tree.

If you pick a persimmon and cut it in
half, you can see the shape of a star.
Every time you see a star,
inside a persimmon or in the sky,
you see the beauty of nature.

▲ the shape of a star in a cross
section of a persimmon

This is the story of a little persimmon tree and the stars in the sky. It is a story of the beauty of nature.

A long time ago, there was a little wood, full of trees.
There were all kinds of trees.
There were big and small trees, green and brown trees, and thick and thin trees.
Animals lived under them, and birds made nests in the branches.
It was a peaceful wood; there were no loud noises.

KEY WORDS

- persimmon
- shiny
- pick
- in half
- shape
- beauty
- a long time ago
- all kinds of
- thick
- thin
- nest
- peaceful
- loud
- noise

The only sounds were the song of the birds, the rustle of
the wind through the trees, and the ripple of the water
in the stream.

The only sounds were natural sounds.

In the summer, the trees had green leaves.

In the autumn, there were fruits and berries.

Birds ate some of the fruits and berries, and squirrels ate
others.

Some of the fruits and berries fell onto the ground.

Then, the leaves changed color and fell onto the ground,
too.

There were brown and golden leaves on the ground
in the wood.

There were seeds from the fruits on the ground in the
wood.

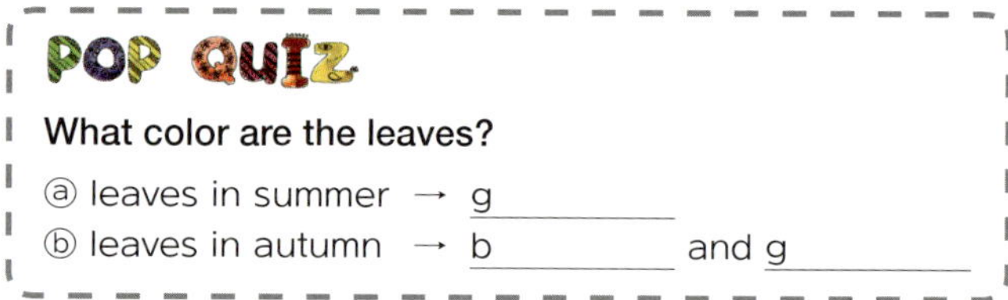

KEY WORDS

- rustle
- ripple
- berry
- squirrel
- fall onto (fall-fell-fallen)
- ground

One little seed fell onto the ground. Leaves and dust
covered it.

In the winter, snow covered the little seed, and it slipped
under the earth to keep warm.

In the spring and summer, sunshine and rain kept
the little seed warm and wet.

KEY WORDS

- seed
- dust
- cover
- slip (slip-slipped-slipped)
- keep
- sunshine

The little seed started to grow.
It pushed a green shoot up
through the earth.
The tiny leaves soaked
up the sunlight.
The seed pushed its
roots down into the
earth, and its stalk grew
thicker and stronger.
Over the seasons, the little
seed became a sapling.
The sapling grew into a small but strong tree.

The tree had a place of his own to grow, with a stream
running by just in front of him.
He spread his branches wider and reached higher.

KEY WORDS

▪ push up	▪ grow thicker	▪ grow into	▪ provide
▪ shoot	▪ strong	▪ spread	▪ shade
▪ soak up	▪ over the seasons	▪ wider	▪ fall off
▪ stalk	▪ sapling	▪ reach higher	▪ be covered with

The young branches of the little tree grew strong green leaves in the spring.

Every year in the summer, the leaves provided shade from the hot sun.

Every year in the autumn, the leaves fell off the tree.

Every year in the winter, the branches were covered with snow.

But every year when spring came again, new leaves grew.

Each year, the little tree grew bigger.

Then, one autumn, some shiny orange fruit appeared,
and slowly the leaves dropped off.

The tree had thin brown branches, but every branch had
some orange fruit.

These were persimmons—round, shiny, and full of juice.

When he looked at himself in the water of the stream,
the tree could see how handsome he was.

He looked just like a picture of a tree in a storybook.

He was not too big and not too small.

He had a strong, straight trunk, and his branches grew
into a nice, round shape.

He was a perfect little tree.

He was not just any tree. He was a persimmon tree with
the shiniest and juiciest fruit in the wood. 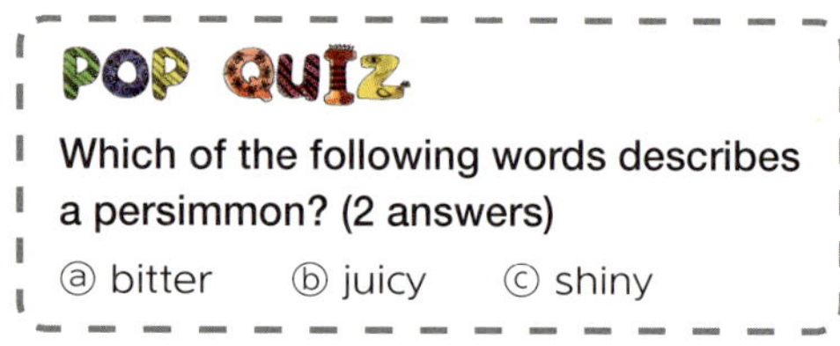

POP QUIZ

Which of the following words describes
a persimmon? (2 answers)

ⓐ bitter   ⓑ juicy   ⓒ shiny

KEY WORDS

• each year	• full of	• straight	• not just any	• melt
• appear	• juice	• trunk	• juicy	
• drop off	• handsome	• perfect	• bare	

On each branch, there were big orange persimmons.

The animals and birds ate the shiny juicy persimmons,

until the branches were bare once again.

Only the snow and ice of the winter covered the branches

of the tree.

Then, in the spring, the snow melted, and new leaves

appeared.

For several years, the life of the little tree was peaceful.

The animals and birds of the wood enjoyed his fruit.

It was quiet and safe in the middle of the wood.

Then, one year, a little boy arrived. He came in
the spring and climbed the tree.

He played in the branches of the tree.

KEY WORDS

- for several years
- quiet
- safe
- in the middle of
- arrive
- climb
- swing (swing-swung-swung)
- jump down
- wave goodbye
- whenever

He swung up into the tree and jumped down to the
ground.
He came in the summer, sat in the shade under
the leaves of the tree, and read his picture books.
He came back in the autumn and picked the sweet juicy
persimmons.
He cut the juicy fruit in half to see the shape of the star.
He sat and ate the fruit until he could see the stars in
the sky.
Then, it was time for him to go home. He waved
goodbye to the tree.
The tree waved his branches and leaves.
Whenever the boy came to the wood, the little tree was
happy.

POP QUIZ

Fill in the blanks with the right seasons.

ⓐ in the __________ → The boy climbed the tree.
ⓑ in the __________ → The boy sat in the shade under the tree.
ⓒ in the __________ → The boy ate the persimmons.

Chapter One · Comprehension Quiz

A Which of the following words describes a persimmon? (2 answers)

perfect

ugly

huge

wrong

funny

handsome

B Mark T for true or F for false.

❶ Squirrels and birds ate the fruit on the trees.   T F

❷ The wood was a very noisy and scary place.   T F

❸ In the spring, there were fruits and berries on the trees.   T F

❹ The little seed grew into a persimmon tree.   T F

C Choose the best answer to each question.

❶ What shape were the tree's branches?

a) 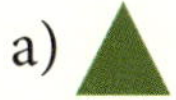   b)    c)    d) 

❷ What was special about the little tree?

a) It had green leaves in summer.

b) It was a persimmon tree with shiny, juicy orange fruit.

c) Its leaves fell off in winter.

d) Its leaves changed color in autumn.

D Solve the crossword puzzle with the right word for each blank.

> **Where did the little tree grow?**

→ The l ❶ ______ t ❷ ______ g ❸ ______ by the
s ❹ ______ in the w ❺ ______ .

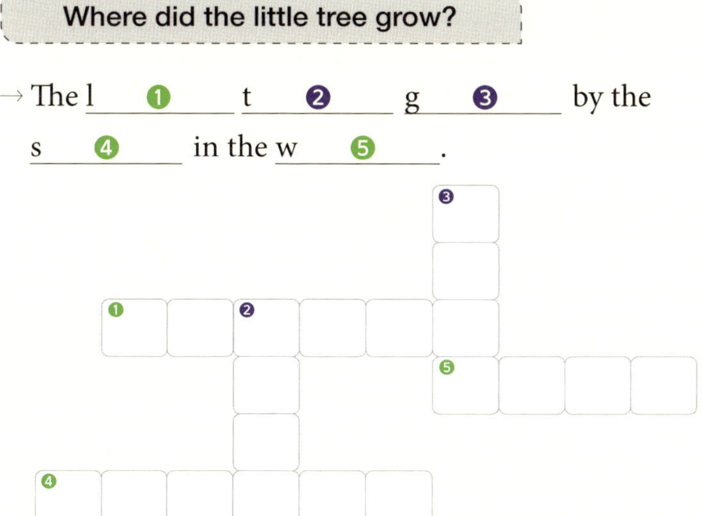

The Little Boy

One day, the little boy came to the wood as usual. But this time his family came, too.

His father and mother came, and the little boy showed them the tree.

They looked at the tree, and walked around.

But they were not interested in the tree. 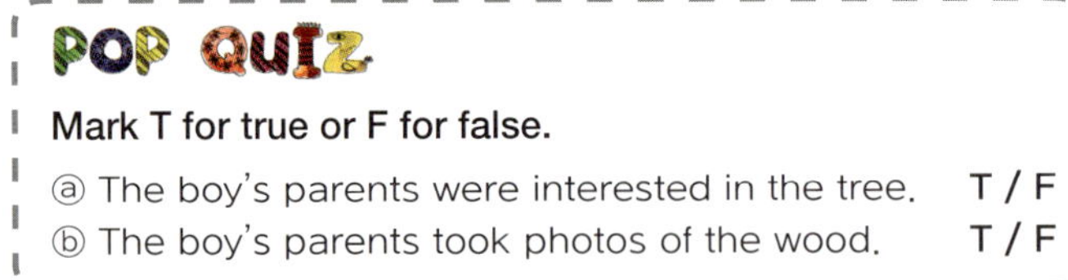

They looked at all of the other trees, and they took photos.

The tree tried to smile with his branches for the photos.

But it is hard for a tree to smile. Even so, the little boy smiled back at the tree.

POP QUIZ

Mark T for true or F for false.

ⓐ The boy's parents were interested in the tree.   T / F
ⓑ The boy's parents took photos of the wood.   T / F

He climbed up, until his mother and father told him
he could not go so high.
When it was time for them to go home, he turned and
waved at the tree, and the tree waved his branches.

- as usual
- show
- walk around
- be interested in
- take photos
- even so
- turn

They came back again later in the year, when the snow
was on the ground.

The tree's branches were white with frost and ice, and
sparkled in the winter sun.

KEY WORDS

- later
- frost
- sparkle
- as well
- shouting

- **chop down** (chop-chopped-chopped)
- axe
- saw
- into pieces
- take away

The boy's mother and father walked around the wood again.

Again, they took photos.

Again, the tree tried to smile.

The next time they came, some people came as well.

The wood was full of noises and shouting.

They cut down other trees in the wood.

Every day, the people chopped down a new tree.

They cut through the wood with axes and saws. 

The trees fell, and they cut them into small pieces.

Then, the people put all of the pieces of wood on big trucks and took them away.

For a while the little tree was frightened.

Every day, he watched the people cutting and digging.

One by one, the trees in the wood were cut down.

There were empty spaces in the wood where the trees had been.

But they did not cut the little tree down.

They made lines and dug ditches in the space where the other trees had been, and they started to build.

More trucks came with bricks and metal and glass.

They crashed and banged and drilled. They built walls and fences and roads through the wood.

They built a house right next to the little tree.

When they had finished, there was a shiny new house, with a green roof and big glass windows.

The tree watched all of this and wondered what was going to happen.

KEY WORDS

- for a while
- dig (dig-dug-dug)
- one by one
- cut down
- empty
- space
- ditch
- build (build-built-built)
- brick
- metal
- glass
- crash
- bang
- drill
- fence
- next to
- finish
- wonder

POP QUIZ
Match the two halves of the sentences.
ⓐ The people   ・   ・ ① was frightened.
ⓑ The little tree   ・   ・ ② a house.
ⓒ They built   ・   ・ ③ chopped down some trees.

Then, one day, the boy who liked the tree came to live in
the house with his mother and father.

He played by the tree every day. His friends came too,
and together they climbed up the tree.

They swung from its branches, and swam in the stream
that ran by just in front of the tree.

They tied a rope to one of the branches, and swung out
over the stream.

Sometimes they let go of the rope and splashed into
the stream.

In the autumn, they picked the fruit.

They cut the fruit in half, and looked at the shape of
the star.

In the winter, when the stream froze, they came and
played on the ice.

Once again, the life of the tree was peaceful.

The only sounds now were the wind in the leaves, the
song of the birds, and the voices of the children playing.

The little persimmon tree missed the other trees, but he
enjoyed the company of the boy and his friends.

KEY WORDS

- **run** (run-ran-run)
- **in front of**
- **rope**
- **let go of** (let-let-let)
- **splash**
- **freeze** (freeze-froze-frozen)
- **voice**
- **miss**
- **enjoy**
- **the company of**

When the boy grew older, his family moved away.

His father and mother packed everything into big boxes.

The boy packed his boxes too, and he waved to the tree before they drove away in their car.

The little tree looked at the empty house. He looked at the sky.

He missed the trees from the wood, and now he missed the little boy, too.

For a time, the little house was empty. But then more people came with machines.

The noise was even louder than before. Machines drilled and dug and hammered.

The machines knocked down the little house, and they built big new buildings.

They were huge buildings, made of metal and concrete and glass.

The new buildings reached high up into the sky.

KEY WORDS

- **grow older** (grow-grew-grown)
- **move away**
- **pack**
- **drive away** (drive-drove-driven)
- **machine**
- **louder**
- **knock down**
- hammer
- huge
- made of
- modern
- at first
- block
- **feel very small** (feel-felt-felt)

The little tree had never seen buildings so big and modern and shiny.

At first, he was excited that he found himself in the middle of a modern city.

But the buildings blocked the sun, so the little tree could not see it anymore.

On each side of the little tree were big buildings reaching high up into the sky.

The little tree felt very small.

A Solve the crossword puzzle with the right word for each blank.

→ They built a b **1** _______ m **2** _______ c **3** _______
with lots of h **4** _______ b **5** _______ in it.

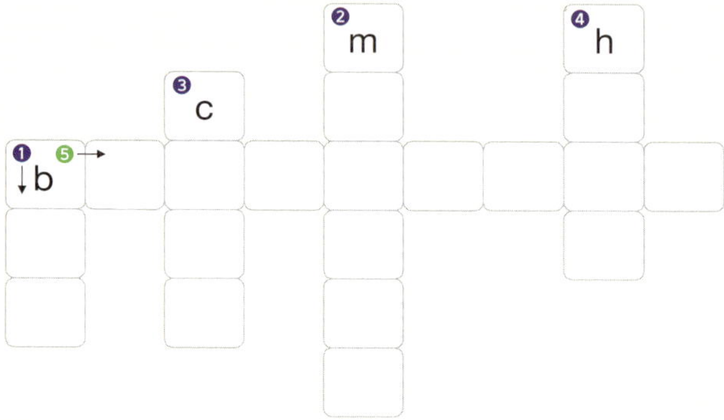

B Mark T for true or F for false.

1 One spring, a little boy came and played in the tree.   T F

2 The little boy didn't like the taste of the persimmons.   T F

3 Some people came and cut down the little tree.   T F

4 The tree liked the boy and his friends.   T F

  Choose the best answer to each question.

❶ What did the little boy and his friends do in the stream?

a) crashed and banged   b) swam and splashed

c) climbed and jumped   d) watched and waited

❷ Why did the people cut some of the trees down?

a) They didn't like the trees.

b) They thought there were too many trees.

c) The trees had a disease.

d) They were clearing a space to build a house.

D Put the sentences in order.

❶ The little boy brought his parents, and they took photos of the wood.

❷ Some people came and built a house.

❸ They came back in the winter and took more photos.

❹ The boy and his family came to live in the house.

_______ → _______ → _______ → _______

The Beautiful Park

Hundreds of people came to live in the big buildings.
Every day, people rushed past the tree on their way to
work. They chattered and shouted.

They got into cars, buses, and trains, which made
the place very noisy again.

More machines came to dig and to drill. The machines
were very noisy too.

The machines built a big road right in front of the tree.
The road covered the stream.

Cars and buses filled the big road.

The branches of the tree swayed every time a truck
thundered past.

KEY WORDS

- rush past
- on one's way to work
- chatter
- shout

- get into
- noisy
- sway
- thunder

- past
- on top of
- tower
- hold up

Then, the machines came back, and they built another
road right on top of the first one.
There were big towers of concrete holding up the top
highway.
The top highway blocked the sunlight even more.

At night-time, it blocked the view of the stars in the sky.

It blocked the air, too, and even more cars and buses rushed past.

The air was filled with smoke, and the leaves of the tree grew dirty.

The tree still grew his new leaves in spring. But they quickly got dirty, too.

In the autumn, he still had shiny orange persimmons, and birds still came to peck at the fruit.

But the tree missed the other trees, the animals, and the little boy.

He missed the peace and quiet. He missed the stars. He missed the fresh air.

For years, the little tree was sad, since it was in the
shadows of the big buildings and the big highways.
The dirt from all of the cars covered the little tree.
The noise of the cars, buses, and highway battered
the little tree.
Nobody climbed up the tree. Nobody took photos of
the tree.
Nobody even stopped to look at the tree.
The tree got older and older and dirtier and dirtier. 
His branches drooped down.

POP QUIZ

What happened to the little tree's leaves in spring?
ⓐ They became dirty.
ⓑ They stopped growing.

Then, one day in autumn, an old man came along. His
legs were slow, and he was bent over.

His hair was white, and he had a stick to help him walk.

He looked up at the little tree. When the tree saw his
face, he knew who it was.

The tree saw that it was the little boy. Only now, he had
grown old, too.

The old man smiled at the tree. He took a photo of the
tree, and the tree smiled back.

He came up to the tree, and touched it gently.

The branches of the little tree swayed.

He picked a juicy persimmon, cut it in half, and saw
the shape of the star.

POP QUIZ
Who was the visitor?
ⓐ the little boy from many years ago
ⓑ the little boy's father

KEY WORDS

- **bite into** (bite-bit-bitten)
- **delicious**
- **last**
- **a piece of**
- **left**
- **make sure that** (make-made-made)

He bit into the orange fruit. It was just as delicious as
he remembered. 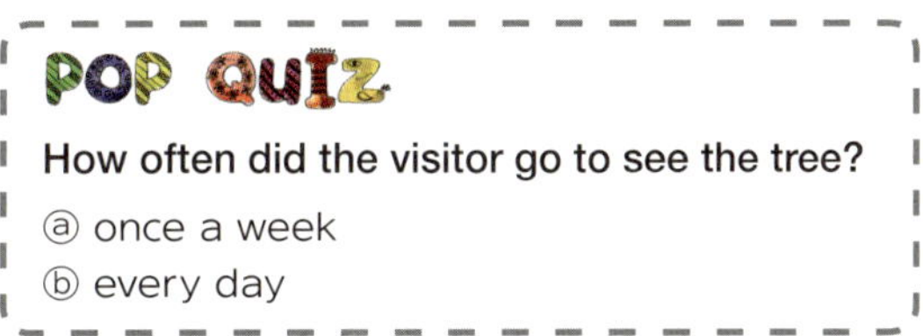
He looked up at the branches of the tree.
Up on one branch, there was an old piece of rope.
It was the last piece of rope left on the tree that
the children used to swing on over the stream.
The old man looked at the rope and remembered.
"Don't you worry, my friend," he said to the tree.
"I am going to make sure that you are happy again."
Then, he sat down just in front of the tree and wrote
something in a big book.
After that, he came back to see the tree every day.

POP QUIZ

How often did the visitor go to see the tree?

ⓐ once a week
ⓑ every day

One day, he brought some other people with him, and
they walked around and looked at the highway and back
at the tree.

KEY WORDS

- **bring** (bring-brought-brought)
- **important**
- **smart**
- briefcase
- measure
- busily

They were important men and women in smart clothes, with briefcases, computers, and phones.

They measured and they talked busily. They looked up and down.

They looked at the cars and trucks rushing by.

They looked at the concrete towers and the tall buildings.

They looked at the tree, and typed words into their computers.

They drew pictures on their computers.

When it got dark, the old man pointed up into the sky.

They all looked up in the sky, but they could not see the stars.

Match the two halves of the sentences.

ⓐ The men and women •   • ① they could not see the stars.
ⓑ They drew   •   • ② wore smart clothes.
ⓒ When they looked up •   • ③ pictures on their computers.

KEY WORDS

- type words
- draw (draw-drew-drawn)
- get dark
- point up

Then, the next day, they brought machines.

These machines were even bigger than the machines that had come before.

The tree watched sadly. He thought they were going to build even more roads and buildings.

But this time, the machines started to pull down the big highway.

They pulled down the big buildings. They took all the pieces away on trucks.

They uncovered the little stream. The sunlight shone on the running water.

Next to the stream, they dug down into the ground, and they planted flowers.

On the other side of the stream, they planted seeds, and new little trees started to grow.

POP QUIZ
What did the big machines do?
ⓐ They built another highway.
ⓑ They pulled down the highway and buildings.

Next to the stream, there was a pretty pathway, and
people began to walk along it.

Soon, every morning, people walked along the pathway
and went past the little tree.

They were happy as they walked, and they always
looked at the little tree and smiled.

There were no cars, no trucks, and no machines.

It was quiet and peaceful again.

Then, animals came, birds came, and fish came in the
stream.

All the time, the little persimmon tree watched.

Every year in the spring, he grew leaves. In the autumn, he had shiny fruit.

But now there were other trees, animals, and the old man.

Now at night-time, they could see the stars again.

Children climbed up the tree.

They swung from his branches and swam in the stream.

In the autumn, they picked the juicy fruit.

And people stopped and smiled at the pretty little tree with his shiny orange fruit.

KEY WORDS
- pathway
- walk along

Chapter Three Comprehension Quiz

A Choose all the expressions that describe the city where the persimmon tree lives.

noisy traffic

smoky, dirty air

beautiful trees

colorful flowers

lots of busy people

quiet and peaceful

B Fill in each blank with the right word below.

dug   pulled   uncovered   planted

❶ They _______________ down the big highway and buildings.

❷ They _______________ the little stream.

❸ They _______________ into the ground and _______________ flowers and trees.

C Choose the best answer to each question.

❶ Who did the old man bring with him to see the tree?

   a) his mother and father   b) his friends

   c) another old man   d) some people in smart clothes

❷ Why did the old man bring the other people to see the tree?

   a) So they could climb it

   b) So they could build more roads and buildings

   c) So they could design a beautiful park in the city

   d) So they could cut it down

D Put the sentences in order.

❶ They knocked down the highway and built a beautiful park around the tree.

❷ He brought lots of important people with smart clothes and computers.

❸ The people in the city enjoyed the park, and the little tree was happy again.

❹ The little boy came back when he had grown into an old man.

_______ → _______ → _______ → _______

Let's Review the Story

Fill in the blanks to review the story.

Title: __________

Story 1: The __________

Place: __________ __________, a beautiful island in the sea

Main Characters: Ji-hye, Ji-hye's __________, Ji-hye's __________

Sequence:
1) Ji-hye receives a __________ __________ on her __________ birthday.
2) Her __________ says she can go diving but tells her to be careful.
3) The first time she tries to dive, her mouth fills up with __________ __________.
4) The __________ time, her mouth fills up with __________ __________ again.
5) The __________ time, she brings back some __________.
6) Now she understands how h__________ it is to be a __________.

Story 2: The __________

Place: A little __________ full of trees

Main Characters: The little __________, the little __________

Sequence:
1) A little __________ tree grew in a wood.
2) A __________ boy and his family came to __________ in a little house in the wood.
3) __________ came and cut down __________.
4) They built a big noisy c__________ around the __________ __________.
5) The __________ __________ came back when he was an __________ man.
6) The old man persuaded p__________ to build a __________ __________ around the little tree.

Let's Think & Talk

Think about the following questions and answer them freely.

❶ Since Jeju Island is an island, it has many aspects that are different from inland areas. Tell us what is special about Jeju Island.

❷ We applied for Jeju divers to be designated as a UNESCO World Heritage. Tell us what other Korean heritages have the UNESCO World Heritage designation.

❸ We have four distinctive seasons which are spring, summer, autumn and winter. Tell us what characteristics each season has.

❹ All over the world as cities get bigger and bigger, nature is destroyed to make room for roads and houses. When we destroy nature, how does it affect humans?

Answers — Let's Review the Story

Title: Living with Nature

Story 1: The Grandmother Diver

Place: Jeju Island, a beautiful island in the sea

Main Characters: Ji-hye, Ji-hye's mother, Ji-hye's grandmother

Sequence:

1) Ji-hye receives a diving suit on her eighth birthday.
2) Her mother says she can go diving but tells her to be careful.
3) The first time she tries to dive, her mouth fills up with sea water.
4) The second time, her mouth fills up with sea water again.
5) The third time, she brings back some seaweed.
6) Now she understands how hard it is to be a diver.

Story 2: The Persimmon Tree

Place: A little wood full of trees

Main Characters: The little tree, the little boy

Sequence:

1) A little persimmon tree grew in a wood.
2) A little boy and his family came to live in a little house in the wood.
3) People came and cut down trees.
4) They built a big noisy city around the little tree.
5) The little boy came back when he was an old man.
6) The old man persuaded people to build a beautiful park around the little tree.

After-reading Test

- Living with Nature
- Level 4
- 28 Questions

  (Vocabulary 7 / Reading Comprehension 16 /

  Sentence Structure & Grammar 5)

1. Which of the following has the same meaning with the word "vacation"?
   ① island   ② sea
   ③ holidays   ④ honey

2. Which of the following has the opposite meaning with the word "leave"?
   ① call   ② come back
   ③ watch   ④ play

3. Which of the following is the wrong past tense form of the verb?
   ① picked   ② saw
   ③ bent   ④ bite

※ Choose the right word for each blank. (4~5)

4. She goes into the water and waits ____________ a big wave.

   ① in   ② for
   ③ to   ④ on

5. The top highway ____________ the sunlight even more.

   ① blocked
   ② brought
   ③ caught
   ④ passed

※ Choose the common word for the two blanks. (6~7)

6.
> • The air was ____________ with smoke.
> • Cars and buses ____________ the big road.

① full   ② dive
③ filled   ④ sank

7.
> • They walk down ____________ the beach.
> • Hundreds of people came ____________ live in the big buildings.

① for   ② into
③ so   ④ to

8. When is Ji-hye on Jeju Island?
  ① She is always there.
  ② She goes there on vacation.
  ③ She visits it twice a year.
  ④ She is there during the school year.

9. What does Ji-hye do when she is not busy?
  ① She watches movies.
  ② She goes to the sea.
  ③ She climbs mountains.
  ④ She rides her horse.

10. What does Ji-hye receive for her birthday? (2 answers)
  ① a bag of rice
  ② a book of maps
  ③ a black rubber suit
  ④ swimming goggles

11. What happens when Ji-hye dives beneath the water for the first time?
  ① She pulls up some seaweed.
  ② She catches a fish.
  ③ She grabs a starfish.
  ④ She comes back with nothing.

12. What does Ji-hye's grandmother NOT wear when she goes diving?
  ① goggles
  ② big fins
  ③ an oxygen tank
  ④ a black rubber suit

13. How does Ji-hye feel after she finishes diving?
  ① tired and embarrassed
  ② excited but nervous
  ③ excited and tired
  ④ embarrassed but pleased

14. What does Ji-hye's grandmother tell her?
  ① The sea is dangerous.
  ② She should never dive again.
  ③ Her mother wants her to stay on shore.
  ④ She should be careful of sharks.

15. What is Ji-hye's dream?
  ① to leave Jeju island
  ② to become a diver
  ③ to meet her father
  ④ to work with her mother

16. What shape can you see if you cut a persimmon in half?

① a square

② a triangle

③ a circle

④ a star

17. When were there fruits and berries?

① in spring

② in summer

③ in autumn

④ in winter

18. What did the little seed become after a few seasons?

① a big tree

② a sapling

③ a flower

④ a bush

19. What did the little boy do in the summer?

① He played on the mountain by the little tree.

② He read picture books under the little tree.

③ He built a tree house in the little tree.

④ He put up a tent and slept under the little tree.

20. Who did the little boy show the little tree to?

① his brother and sister

② his mother and father

③ his friends

④ his classmates

21. What did the people who visited do to the other trees in the wood?
 ① They watered the trees.
 ② They picked the trees' fruits.
 ③ They cut down the trees.
 ④ They put lights on the trees.

22. What happened when the little boy grew older?
 ① He and his family moved away.
 ② Only the little boy moved away.
 ③ Only the little boy's parents moved away.
 ④ More of his family members moved into the house.

23. Who visited the little tree one day in autumn?
 ① an old man
 ② an old woman
 ③ a young boy
 ④ a young girl

24. Choose the wrong part of the sentence.

> <u>Where</u> she <u>is</u> not busy, she <u>likes</u> to go down <u>to</u> the sea.
>   ①   ②   ③   ④

※ Choose the correct word or phrase for each blank. (25~27)

25.
> She wants Ji-hye to study ____________ she can have a better job.

 ① but　　　　　　　　　② that
 ③ so that　　　　　　　④ so much

26.
> It was just as delicious __________ he remembered.

① than   ② as
③ better   ④ so

27.
> They cut through the wood __________ axes and saws.

① with   ② as
③ in   ④ to

28. Choose the correct sentence.
    ① But they were not interesting in the tree.
    ② But they were not interested in the tree.
    ③ But they don't interested in the tree.
    ④ But they did not interested in the tree.

Memo

Memo 

Memo

Memo

Peter Wynne-Willson & Ruth Wilson

Peter Wynne-Willson is a playwright and theatre director from Birmingham, UK. He has written more than forty plays, mostly for young audiences, including "The Bridge", "Heads or Tails" and "Roy". He was Artistic Director of Big Brum Theatre-in-Education Company from 1982-92, and Visiting Professor of Theatre-in-Education at the Korean National University of the Arts 1999-2005.

Ruth Wilson is an experienced secondary school teacher and teacher trainer living in Birmingham in the UK. She has a Diploma in Teaching English to Speakers of Other Languages (TESOL) in Further, Adult and Community Education, a Master's Degree (MEd) in Human Rights and Equality and a Doctorate of Education (EdD) in Education Policy. She is currently working for the British Council on their EAL Nexus project.

Living with Nature

Written by Peter Wynne-Willson, Ruth Wilson
Illustrated by Jungho Joung

First Published in December 2014

Editorial Manager: Juyon Choi
Editors: Juyon Choi, Jeeyoung Kim, Kyunghee Jang, Jiyeong Park
Designers: Eunhee Lee, Elim
Cover Designer: Eunhee Lee

Published and distributed by

Darakwon Bldg., 64-1 Jandari-ro, Mapo-gu, Seoul, Korea 121-894
Tel: 82-2-736-2031(ext. 250)   Fax: 82-2-736-2037
Homepage: www.ihappyhouse.co.kr
Publisher: Kyudo Chung

ISBN: 978-89-6653-164-6 18740 / 978-89-6653-156-1 18740(set)

[Components]
• 1 Audio CD (Recording Studio: Aram)
• Answer Keys & Korean Translation: Free download at www.ihappyhouse.co.kr